Christianity, A Religion Of Facts, Not Of Speculation: Being The First Of A Series Of Nine Discourses

George Greenwell

In the interest of creating a more extensive selection of rare historical book reprints, we have chosen to reproduce this title even though it may possibly have occasional imperfections such as missing and blurred pages, missing text, poor pictures, markings, dark backgrounds and other reproduction issues beyond our control. Because this work is culturally important, we have made it available as a part of our commitment to protecting, preserving and promoting the world's literature. Thank you for your understanding.

CHRISTIANITY

A RELIGION OF FACTS,

NOT OF SPECULATION,

BEING THE

FIRST OF A SERIES OF NINE DISCOURSES

DELIVERED IN

SOUTH BRIDGE HALL, EDINBURGH.

By GEORGE GREENWELL.

EDINBURGH:
PHILIP CADELL GRAY, NORTH BRIDGE:
SIMPKIN, MARSHALL & CO. LONDON;
AND T. KIRK, NOTTINGHAM.

1843.

The subjects of the remaining Discourses are as follow:

2d.—Credibility of the Witnesses.
3d.—Provisions of Christianity in harmony with the Intellectual and Moral Structure of Man.
4th.—Overthrow of Paganism by Primitive Christianity.
5th.—Nature and Criteria of Miracles.
6th.—Nature and Evidence of Prophecy.
7th.—Signs of the Times in reference to the Advance of Popery, Infidelity, and all the Agencies of Evil.
8th.—Man a Free Agent.
9th.—Man a Responsible Being.

Should the First be encouraged, the Second will be hastened through the Press; and, depending upon the same condition, the whole of the series will follow.

CHRISTIANITY

A RELIGION OF FACTS, &c.

TRUTH is the breath of God, and where He breathes there is life, health, and peace. Falsehood is the breath of the Evil One, the enemy of God and man, and where he breathes there is discord, disease, and death. But though the myriads of our fallen race have desperately battled against truth, age after age, compelling the heavenly visitant to prophesy in sackcloth, and mourn in the desert, with harp on the willows, yet truth remains. Though exquisite in loveliness, she is not frail, like the fair ones of earth; but strong and indestructible from her nature and constitution.

Truth is the great want of man. It is celestial food adapted to his nature, and without it his life is but a complication of maladies. Without truth, men are but hordes of animals,—cruel, selfish, tormented and enslaved, preying upon each other, and lacerating themselves. Without truth, the world is a wide, weary, tangled waste; and even home is barren, joyless, and unsanctified. Without truth, the marvellous temple of nature appears but a huge prison-house,—a dark and noisome dungeon, into which we have been cast by some merciless tyrant for the punishment of some unknown sin. The resplendent rivers may run in brightness beneath the sun; the cataracts may fall in sheeted silver, or fountains may spout in music under the shade of the sycamore, yet all is discord. The hills may rise like pathways into heaven; the fields may laugh out in the exuberance of joy; the glens may smile in the solemn beauty of old romance; yet all is barren! But give us truth, and the hovel is a palace, and the world an Eden;

for truth is the parent of love, liberty, peace, light, joy, and hope. Oh truth! thou fairest emanation of the Holy One, Immortal, Benevolent, ill-used pilgrim of the world, lead us to thy hallowed fane and we will bow in lowliest abasement; for the lower we fall under thy influence, the higher we rise towards heaven and God. Bring us to that consecrated prophetic grove which is thy serene retreat; and let us drink in largess from thy undefiled wells, and bathe our soiled and heated spirits in the renovating streams which mumur there in such placid melody.—Hasten, or we die!

All truth is valuable, and man is ennobled in proportion as he thirsts after truth on all subjects. But that truth which has reference to the supremacy of the moral man, and the eternity of such a condition, must necessarily be of the highest kind, and claim the most engrossing interest. Christianity is *the truth*, by way of eminence; being a full disclosure concerning the character of God—the nature of man, and the relation which subsists between them. A grand remedial scheme for the reconciliation of an apostate and wandering race; proposing to secure to them the pardon of all past guilt, and the undisturbed possession of more than their original felicity. But, to approach more closely to the subject of the present lecture, Christianity is not only truth of the highest kind, but truth in the most awakening shape. Facts have moral and spiritual power which abstract truth possesses not. Hence, when any important truth is enshrined in a fact, when it is embodied in deeds, and thus rendered palpable in the living world, it finds readier access to the understanding, the conscience, and the affections, and has more impulsive power than it could have in any other form. To illustrate this matter, we shall remark that—If the angels that stand in the presence of God had come down to earth and spoken to men in the music of heaven,—if they had attempted to convince the human family that sin is a fearful thing in the sight of God; so dire and malignant in its nature and consequences, that He cannot look upon it with any degree of allowance: And if they had attempted, at the same time, to convince our race, that though God hates sin, yet, being the Creator and Father of us all, He loves us with an overflowing love, and yearns over his children. Had the angelic beings attempted to make these two truths clear to us from the reason and nature of things, we might have been silenced perhaps, but we should neither have been enlightened nor consoled. Though it is no paradox in statement, yet it would have been one in action;—when we had begun to think upon the bitterness and the evil of sin considered as rebellion against God, our minds would have been so torn by anguish, and crushed by despair, that the fair idea of His overflowing love could not have entered or existed in us at the same time. On the other hand, if we had cherished the idea of His unbroken love, and thought of God as of a Father of great indulgence, always yearning over his children, our conceptions of the guilt of sin would have been slight and disproportionate; and thus we should have abandoned ourselves to licentiousness in the dream of mercy, and lived in sin amid the visions of heaven.

But when Christ, the brightness of the Divine glory, and the express image of His person, divested himself of his regal honours, and came out from the imperial splendour in a body of flesh,—when he humbled himself, by taking the nature and likeness of sinful flesh, and in that body became a victim for the sins of the world,—when the Son of God hung upon a bloody cross with common malefactors,—a spectacle to men and angels—to heaven, earth, and hell,—then the two abstract truths, which angels could not have taught with efficiency, were embodied and harmonised in a fact of astonishing import, and incalculable power. If sin had not been much more malignant and hideous than we commonly imagine, it might have been expiated by a meaner sacrifice than the blood of God's own dear Son. And if the love of God towards the fallen had not been richer and deeper than human or angelic thought can reach, that great sacrifice would never have been offered for the life of the world. It was no wonder that the effulgent orb of day refused to shine on such a spectacle; leaving the face of nature covered with a pall of blackness, or that the very rocks became instinct with mysterious life, and shuddering, rent in sunder! for that scene exhibited the fearful nature of sin in all the intensity of its undisguised **loathsomeness**. Nor was it wonderful that the dead saints should be startled out of the slumber of ages, to look upon the great work transpiring; for they were but the types of that new life, which, through the boundless love of God the Father, was rendered accessible by the death of the Holy One.

Had the same angelic beings, of whom we have spoken, come down among men who were dimly and darkly looking forward to the future, haunted by the fear of death, and tortured by the alternate furies of annihilation or despair. Had they reasoned with us that God would never create any thing so glorious in vain—that with our marvellous faculties of body and mind, we must be destined for endless existence, and could not utterly perish in the waste and horrible abyss. By reasoning from this, and many kindred topics with their immense ability, they might have silenced us; but they never could have given us any strength of confidence, or inspiration of hope.—Death would still have been here in all its gloomy realities, and all beyond it covered with clouds and darkness. But the truth on this subject has likewise been embodied in a most astounding fact. It became palpable by the resurrection of the Son of God in power and glory. When we see Him, who represented humanity, arising up in the strength of God from an apparent overthrow,—tearing away the scorpion sting from the monster, on his own dominons,—ascending to the throne of universal empire, amid the acclamation of heaven's enraptured hosts,—scattering down blessings of every kind to the human family—then, indeed, we feel that death is abolished, and immortality brought to light by the gospel; the hope of eternal existence gathers life, power, and distinctness, by having something palpable and definite to rest upon and spring from.

Suffer me, now, to read for exposition and illustration, a portion of the living oracles contained in Paul's epistle to Corinth, 15th chap. " Moreover, brethren, I declare unto you the gospel which I preached unto you, which also ye have received, and wherein ye stand; by which also ye are saved, if ye keep in memory what I preached unto you, unless ye have believed in vain. For

I delivered unto you first of all that which I also received, how that Christ died for our sins according to the scriptures; and that he was buried, and that he rose again the third day according to the scriptures: and that he was seen of Cephas, then of the twelve: after that, he was seen of above five hundred brethren at once; of whom the greater part remain unto this present, but some are fallen asleep. After that he was seen of James; then of all the apostles. And last of all he was seen of me also, as of one born out of due time. For I am the least of the apostles, that am not meet to be called an apostle, because I persecuted the church of God. But by the grace of God I am what I am: and his grace which was bestowed upon me was not in vain; but I laboured more abundantly than they all: yet not I, but the grace of God which was with me. Therefore, whether it were I or they, so we preach, and so ye believed. Now, if Christ be preached that he rose from the dead, how say some among you that there is no resurrection of the dead? But if there be no resurrection of the dead, then is Christ not risen: and if Christ be not risen, then is our preaching vain, and your faith is also vain. Yea, and we are found false witnesses of God: because we have testified of God that he raised up Christ; whom he raised not up, if so be that the dead rise not. For if the dead rise not, then is not Christ raised: and if Christ be not raised, your faith is vain; ye are yet in your sins. Then they also which are fallen asleep in Christ are perished. If in this life only we have hope in Christ, we are of all men most miserable." This is the solemn language of one who possessed a majestic intellect, consecrated by the indwelling of truth, devoted to the most sublime work, and specially illuminated by the inspiration of the Holy Spirit. From being a virulent unrelenting persecutor, he had been arrested, and transformed by the moral power of striking and conclusive evidence, into a champion of that truth which he once despised and vilified. In the chapter which we have read, he is warning a faction of the Corinthian church, who, beguiled by vain philosophy, were doubting or denying the resurrection from the dead. Having reminded them of the historic facts which constituted the foundation of Christianity:—the death, burial, and resurrection of Christ, and likewise of the ample number of veracious witnesses, who beheld the Lord after he rose from the grave; he then comes close to their reason, conscience, and affections, by solemn, masculine, earnest argument.

1. "Now, if Christ be preached that he rose from the dead, how say some among you that there is no resurrection of the dead? But if there be no resurrection of the dead, then is Christ not risen: And if Christ be not risen, then is our preaching vain, and your faith is also vain." This would fall with startling emphasis upon their minds, for none of them doubted the resurrection of Christ, only they were not aware of the fearful consequences of their own doctrine. Nor did they perceive the inseparable connexion between the resurrection of Christ, and that of his people and the world. The apostle's argument would show them with ghastly distinctness, that the principle which they had adopted, rendered the apostolic proclamation, and their own faith, all delusion and vanity; because it involved as the premises that the Lord of life was still the prisoner of the grave,—the victim, and not the conqueror of death.

2. He proceeds to show them that, according to their theory, the proclamation of the gospel was not merely vanity, but likewise infamy. "Yea, and we are found false witnesses of God: because we have testified of God that he raised up Christ; whom he raised not up, if so be that the dead rise not. For if the dead rise not, then is not Christ raised." If the Corinthians were not dead to every fine and generous emotion, they would naturally conclude,—We will renounce this pernicious speculation of ours, for these holy men, who so scrupulously abstain from false witness against their brethren or the world, would never outrage their own moral nature, and incur the wrath of heaven, by bearing false witness concerning God. Such conduct would be utterly inexplicable by the principles of human action.

3. "And if Christ be not risen, your faith is vain, ye are yet in your sins." This was an appeal to their own experience, and surely it would have amazing weight in the chain of his demonstration. The Corin-

thians would be constrained to follow out his argument thus :—" These ambassadors from God declared, that Christ, after his resurrection from the grave, was exalted on high as a Prince and a Saviour, to grant repentance and remission of sins. We believed their testimony, confirmed as it was by mighty signs and wonders, were baptized into the death of Christ, and rose again into life, by receiving at that time the consciousness of pardon—the answer of a good conscience—the seal of Sonship in the family of God. But if, as we have perversely argued, there is no resurrection of the dead, then we are appalled by the conclusion that Christ is not risen. And if Christ be not risen, he cannot be exalted, to give repentance and remission of sins. And if there be no remission of sins, then the testimony was false, the evidence delusion, our faith baseless, and all our new-born emotions of peace, love, and joy, however pure, lofty, and sanctified they might seem, have all been visionary—the veriest phantoms of temporary frenzy! We dare not belie our own experience in this weighty matter,—we give our speculation to the winds, —the Christ who died for our sins has risen again for our justification ; and in his salvation we will evermore rejoice with joy unspeakable and full of glory."

4. " Then they who are fallen asleep in Christ are perished." To such of these Sadducean philosophers as had committed to the house of desolation their Christian friends and brethren, this would open an abyss of fearful melancholy. The tenderness of their old associations would rise up in rebellion against the hardness and insensibility of their new philosophy. They would bury their monstrous speculation in the grave of terror which arose before them, exclaiming, with the thrill of returning conviction and growing confidence, Now is Christ risen from the dead, and become the first fruits of them that slept!

5. The apostle continues, " If the dead rise not, why stand we in jeopardy every hour. I protest, by your rejoicing in Christ, I die daily. If, after the manner of men, I have fought with beasts at Ephesus, what advantageth it me, if the dead rise not ?" This would open another field of earnest thought to all whose hearts

were not seared beyond redemption. The apostle's argument would lead them into a track of this kind:—These men cannot be bearing false witness, because it is manifest that they have no ambitious or interested motives. In proclaiming their message to the world, they have to buffet the torrent of worldly passion—to endure the tortures of varied and fierce persecution—to abide the sardonic sneers of philosophy and literature. They are counted as the filth and offscouring of all things, and have to welter in the very mire of infamy. Nor are they suffering these things in promulgating any opinions of their own or other men, but in bearing testimony to great and sensible facts, so notorious that their most rancorous enemies can find no hostile or conflicting evidence. They cannot be courting misery and anguish here, and at the same time accumulating wrath hereafter. They cannot dream that the testimony which has lost them this world, if it be false, will gain them the world to come! No—they are, indeed, the witnesses of God, and the ambassadors of heaven. We will cling to their doctrine, cherish their hope, breathe their love, and pray for an inspiration of the same moral heroism and divine fortitude. The sting of death is sin, and the strength of sin is the law; but, thanks be to God, who giveth us the victory, through our Lord Jesus Christ.

Having briefly analyzed this portion of the apostolic word, suffer me now, in a more extended way, to examine the meaning or import of the wonderful facts on which Christianity reposes:—

1st, Public justice required, either that an atonement should be made, or that the law should be executed upon every offender. By public justice, I mean that due administration of law which secures in the highest manner attainable all private and public interests among rational and moral agents, preserving the order and wellbeing of the whole intelligent universe. It is not hard to conceive that the interest of that great moral empire, at the head of which God reigns as supreme lawgiver, might require that his abhorrence of sin should be solemnly testified by a tremendous sacrifice. Sin is not a private offence, or it might be blotted out without any severe inquisition, or public and govermental solemnities. Sin is a public offence,—it is revolt against the supremacy of God, outrage against the relations in which we stand to all orders of being, and foul dishonour to the majesty of those laws, by which the happiness of moral agents can alone be secured. Hence, in blotting out sin through the humiliation, death and intercession of one so elevated in the scale of being, at the same time that sin is remitted, and sinners reconciled to God, the character of God is successfully vindicated, the law is magnified and made honourable, the offender is humbled and prostrated into his proper place, whilst all classes of being in the rational universe can rejoice that the spirit of law has been preserved inviolate, without the execution of its letter.

2d, An atonement was called for in refutation of Satanic slander. In seducing our original parents from their allegiance, this great enemy of God and man imputed selfishness to the Creator;—he insinuated that the knowledge, power, and enjoyment which legitimately belonged to them had been unreasonably curtailed. And, after distrust, unbelief, and disobedience were originated, the selfishness which had been imputed to God, fell upon man in withering blight, and adheres to him as a deadly curse. The sacrifice of Christ is a public and most triumphant refutation of Satan's lie, whilst, at the same time, it is a standing memorial against the selfishness which consumes the world, and crowds with frantic ungodly hosts the dominions of darkness and despair. It is an ocean of pure, disinterested, overwhelming love, too deep and limitless to be sounded or explored by the sons of men, though they may bathe and spring upward into life and immortality. God has been unveiled to the human family in the person and work of Jesus Christ. His nature has been disclosed to us in affluence of tenderness, so that we can concur in the glowing language of the apostle:—" He that spared not his own Son, but delivered him up for us all, how shall he not with him also freely give us all things? Who shall lay anything to the charge of God's elect? It is God that justifieth; who is he that condemneth? It is Christ that died, yea, rather that is risen again, who is even at the right hand of God, who also maketh intercession for us." Rom. ix.

3*d*, An atonement was needed, not to placate or render God merciful, but to remove those obstacles which prevented his love from flowing forth. In the theology of the schools, God has been pourtrayed as a stern vindictive being, whose terrible wrath would have burned down to the lowest hell, had he not been placated or rendered merciful by the death of his own Son. But this is a gross misapprehension of the divine character. God always loved the human family. It is his very nature; but be it remembered, that love would be a mere tumultuous tide of passion, unless it were controlled by justice and directed by wisdom. We are not the only race of beings in the universe, nor are we isolated from the powers and principalities of heavenly places, the inhabitants of the many mansions in our Father's house. So that the relations out of which laws arise, and the sanctions by which laws are guarded, had to be reverenced and enforced, before salvation could be proclaimed to the perishing. In the death of Christ we do not see the indignation of God, either against his Son or the human family; but against sin as the leaven of all disorder and anguish, offensive to the unspotted purity of his nature, and hostile to the happiness of his creatures. "God so loved the world, that he gave his only begotten Son, that whosoever believeth in him might not perish, but have eternal life."—"Herein is love, not that we loved God, but that he loved us, and sent his Son to be the propitiation for our sins."

4*th*, An atonement was called for by the fact, that the rigid execution of law had not been effectual in arresting the progress of rebellion. The angels who kept not their first estate, but sought to introduce the strife and agony of sinful rebellion, even into the heaven of heavens, were hurled down from the height of their glory, into the depths of hell. Yet the angelic punishment did not operate as a warning, dreadful as it was,—it did not prevent the apostacy of another order of beings, nor the pollution of our earth. Had there been no exhibition of God, except the rigid execution of penal law, who can tell but what rebellion might have rushed in whirlwind speed from world to world, until all classes of being had fallen into desolate ruin. But the Godhead arose as it were out of his place, and came forth in such unutterable loveliness, that the plague was stayed, and rebellion smitten down with an effectual blow.

5*th*, The atonement has given such a disclosure of the nature of sin, as we could not have gained through any other channel. In its origin, its nature, its progress and consequences, it is altogether evil ; and our holy Father, whose dominions it threatens to lay waste, cannot look upon it with any degree of allowance. This is manifest from the death of his dear Son, who has condemned sin in the flesh ; and, by this solemn condemnation, placed us in the light of eternity, where we may see it in all its deformity, and learn to loathe it in all its shapes, whatever be the amount of worldly fascination with which our enemy may seek to beguile us.

6*th*, The atonement has furnished the most influential motives to repentance. In the dominions of Nature, we behold the Godhead in the majesty of his eternal power. In the province of moral government, we discern the wisdom of His providence, but in both these departments, there are fearful anomalies to the natural eye,—manifestations which overpower the intellect, and are inscrutable to reason. In redemption, God comes close to the human heart as a Father; we are no longer appalled by His terrible power, or confused by the foldings of His infinite wisdom ; the sublime idea of God becomes, if we may so speak, humanised,—we can lay hold upon it, and it can enter our souls in all its expanding and purifying influence. When Christ was alluding partly to the manner and partly to the moral power of his sacrifice, he exclaimed, "I, if I be lifted up, will draw all men to me," meaning that his crucifixion would give such a wonderful display of Divine love, that all, whose hearts were not utterly seared by the god of this world and the pursuit of sin, would be drawn in that direction —would be lifted up to the cross in adoring wonder, in subdued reverence, and joyous reconciliation. If the man could be found who has carefully read the evangelic record of the life and death of the Lord, and yet never been smitten by sympathy with his work, or bowed before God in penitence, he would deserve to stand forth from among the multitude of living men, that all orders of being might crowd together to gaze upon one so lost to all nobility of soul, and dead to generous feeling.

7th, The atonement has illustrated our capability of advancement in intellectual power and moral consecration. Was God manifest in flesh, that he might reconcile the world to himself? Has the eternal Spirit furnished the most astonishing evidence to demonstrate His divinity to us, that we may be awakened with an authentic message of peace and pardon? Do the angels rejoice in the presence of God over every sinner that repenteth? Is Christ swaying the sceptre of government, that he may prepare mansions for all those who follow him, and finally receive them to himself, to be crowned with glory and immortality? What does all this indicate? Not merely the depth of our present misery and wretchedness, but likewise the height from which we have fallen, and our capability of restoration to our pristine state and privileges; there is greatness in humanity, even in its ruins! The fallen columns, though overgrown with rank weeds, still indicate the ancient magnificence of the temple, and still present the materials for a second building more glorious than the first. The revelation of God in Christ was designed not only to teach man what he is, but what he was, and what he may become, through the mercies of a pardoning God. Awake, then, my hearers,—arise from the sleep of sin and death, that Christ may give you the light of life, and the liberty which He alone can communicate.

Before I leave this branch of the subject, I will glance at the difference between that justification which God proposes, and the justification of man in earthly tribunals. In the 3d chapter of Romans, from the 19th verse, we read as follows:—" Now, we know that what things soever the law saith, it saith to them that are under the law; that every mouth may be stopped, and all the world may become guilty before God. Therefore, by the deeds of the law there shall no flesh be justified in his sight: for by the law is the knowledge of sin. But now the righteousness of God without the law is manifested, being witnessed by the law and the prophets; even the righteousness of God which is by faith of Jesus Christ unto all, and upon all them that believe, for there is no difference; for all have sinned, and come short of the glory of God. Being justified freely by his grace, through the redemption that is in Christ Jesus; whom God hath set forth to be a propitiation through faith in his blood; to declare his righteousness for the remission of sins that are past, through the forbearance of God; to declare at this time his righteousness, that he might be just, and the justifier of him who believeth in Jesus." You have all, no doubt, some acquaintance with the spirit and forms of judicial matters in human societies. When we are accused of violating the laws by which the community is held together in peace and good order, we are arrested by public officers, and summoned to the judgment seat, to undergo serious examination. If the charges against us are substantiated, and guilt brought home to us, the law takes its course in the rigid execution of the penalty by which it is guarded. We are condemned, and we suffer. On the other hand, if the accusations are not proven, and our innocence plainly appears, we are honourably acquitted, and the voice of public sympathy loudly echoes the joy of our liberation. Such is human justification: but how different that justification which God the Supreme Ruler proposes to his rebellious subjects. He has summoned us all to his righteous tribunal, convicted us all of unnatural revolt, and proven us guilty in the presence of men and angels; every mouth has been stopped by the clearness and force of the evidence against us. And then condemnation? Oh no! though all are found guilty of enormous ingratitude, and desperate iniquity, yet the God of grace has such wonderful forbearance, that he has proclaimed to all, pardon and justification through the redemption that is in Christ Jesus, whom he hath set forth to be a propitiation—remission of all past sin, and sonship in the family of God, is accessible to all the human family through his overwhelming favour. Why then should any still continue to crouch before the throne as criminals, while the voice of mercy is sounding in their ears? Give credence to the rich proclamation, and the chains will fall off, the gloom will vanish, the enmity will cease, and the divine liberty of the children of God will be yours for evermore. The pure sunlight of heaven is streaming down; God forbid that you should prefer the darkness and clammy vapours of a dungeon!

Let us likewise survey briefly the difference between human love and the love of Christ. In the fifth chapter of the same Epistle, from the 5th verse, it runs thus: " For when we were yet without strength, in due time Christ died for the ungodly; for scarcely for a righteous man will one die, yet peradventure for a good man some would even dare to die. But God commendeth his love toward us, in that while we were yet sinners Christ died for us. Much more, then, being now justified by his blood, we shall be saved from wrath through him; for if, when we were enemies, we were reconciled to God by the death of his Son, much more, being reconciled, we shall be saved through his life; and not only so, but we also joy in God through our Lord Jesus Christ, by whom we have now received the atonement." In the annals of the world, there are a few bright instances on record of individuals who were ready to die for each other. I will allude to one of them. In ancient times there was an individual of great moral worth condemned to die by the stern mandate of an iron-hearted tyrant. Being at some distance from home, he was of course desirous once more to press his own domestic hearth; to take a long farewell of the wife of his bosom, and the pledges of their love. Before this could be granted, an hostage was required by the tyrant, who might suffer in his room in case he should endeavour to escape. A dear friend cheerfully became the hostage, was incarcerated in his room, and on the third day, which was the given time, brought forth *to* suffer. An immense multitude gathered together; the apparatus of death was prepared; the tyrant and his minister sat to witness the execution, still the condemned arrived not; and the hostage was bitterly taunted for his folly. But he had nobility of soul, he knew that his friend must be detained by some invincible circumstances, and he earnestly implored the official men to hasten the execution, that by his death he might spare one so dear to his family, and so valuable to society. Whilst all were in the agony of suspense, torn by conflicting emotions, suddenly a heavy and rapid tramp was heard, the crowd gave way to a foaming horse, and the friends were clasped in each other's arms. Such was the strength of love that they struggled together as to which of them should die, and such was the moral grandeur of the scene, that even the depraved and brutalized mass of people were broken down in spirit. Sympathy with that imposing spectacle ran like electric fire from heart to heart through all the vast assemblage; the hard rock was smitten, and a goodly river freely gushed forth.

But this love was that of one friend to another; they were united by intellectual and moral qualities; by congeniality of mind and oneness of pursuit. The love of Christ has no parallel; nothing like it in the chronicles of the world. He died for his *enemies!* for those who were alienated from God, betraying truth, dishonouring law, polluting the earth, outraging the heavens, and inflicting every kind of torture and misery upon each other. He died not with the sympathy of those for whom he suffered, but amid their infuriate execration, and bitter mockery. Hence God commendeth his love towards us, in that while we were yet sinners, Christ died for us. From this aspect of his love, we may derive unspeakable joy, for being justified by his blood we shall be saved by his life, for if he died for his enemies, he will surely continue his love in the protection of his friends; hence we joy in God through our Lord Jesus Christ, by whom we have received reconciliation, holding in strength of conviction, that he who has bestowed upon us the most distinguished gift in the universe, will never withhold anything of inferior value.

When Christ was buried, the hopes and destinies of our race were all entombed and suspended there; for had he not risen from that dreary prison-house, all the evidence offered during his ministry would have been rendered void. It would then have been dreadfully manifest that God had not accepted that sacrifice which was offered. His grave would have been the grave of merited infamy, and the human race, whose hopes and aspirations had been kindled for a time, would have been mantled in deeper night; they might have crowded together to that spot in frenzied mockery of the past, and sullen despair of the future. But there was no such triumph in reserve for the powers of sin and hell; the day star was not lost in the ocean bed; it arose again in superior radiance, and still burns on in undiminished brightness. It was not possible that he could be holden, for God's character was to be publicly vindicated, his promises in the prophetic word to be fulfilled, the power of the devil to be destroyed, and the enslaved human family to be triumphantly liberated. There was a great earthquake—the voice of God shook the scene of the death and burial of the Lord,—the Roman veterans who had crushed so many foes, trembled and became like dead men when the mighty angel came down to roll away the stone, and looked upon them with a countenance of severe splendour,—the discomfited powers of hell were yoked to the triumphal car of the ascending Redeemer. Captivity was led captive, and heaven's unnumbered hosts came down in etherial purity to follow in the train of that mighty conqueror who was the first begotten from the dead, and the prince of the kings of the earth. With what voices of commanding melody did they speak on arriving at that sanctuary of unsullied holiness, where the throne of the Eternal is reared. " Lift up your heads, O ye gates, and be ye lifted up, ye everlasting doors, and the king of glory shall come in. Who is this king of glory? The Lord strong and mighty, the Lord mighty in battle. Lift up your heads, O ye gates; even lift them up, ye everlasting doors, and the king of glory shall come in. Who is this king of glory? The Lord of hosts, he is the king of glory.* Having entered the everlasting doors amid the jubilant music, and the adoring reverence of cherubim and seraphim, his Father addressed him in the presence of all the powers and principalities:—" Sit thou at my right hand, until I make thine enemies thy footstool. The Lord shall send the rod of thy strength out of Zion;

* 24th Psalm.

rule thou in the midst of thine enemies. Thy people shall be willing in the day of thy power, in the beauties of holiness from the womb of the morning; thou hast the dew of thy youth. The Lord hath sworn, and will not repent. Thou art a priest for ever after the order of Melchisedec. The Lord at thy right hand shall strike through kings in the day of his wrath."* But if the Lord be risen, crowned, and glorified, what does it import? In the first place, we learn from the Apostle Peter, in his first Epistle, that it is the ground of living hope. " Blessed be the God and Father of our Lord Jesus Christ, who, according to his abundant mercy, hath begotten us again unto a lively hope by the resurrection of Jesus Christ from the dead: to an inheritance incorruptible, undefiled, and that fadeth not away, reserved in heaven for you, who are kept by the power of God, through faith unto salvation, ready to be revealed in the last time." That you may enter fully into the spirit of this passage, bear in mind that the disciples during our Lord's personal ministry had a veil over their eyes; their Jewish prejudices were strong, and their faith was weak; though the Saviour often and solemnly declared both his death and resurrection, yet the statement fell upon slow hearts, where it was neither understood nor retained. Hence, when Christ was crucified and entombed, all the hopes of the disciples were buried in their master's grave; they believed not that he would rise again, hence that desponding language, " We trusted that this was he which should have redeemed Israel." Now, when it was fairly manifest that the Lord was risen indeed, the disciples were begotten again into a living hope; their old hope was a perishing one, too frail to survive any trial. But the hope begotten by the triumph of Christ over the powers of death, was a deathless and impulsive hope which cannot be extinguished, but will burn brighter and brighter unto the perfect day. The object of hope is an inheritance of surpassing richness and stability which cannot be defiled or pass away. The consolation of this hope would be indeed great to those persecuted saints who were

* 110th Psalm.

driven up and down in the wilderness of society—hunted as outlaws from city to city—deprived of friends, property, country, home, and reputation, for the cause of Jesus Christ. By strong faith and vivid hope, they apprehended the salvation which is to be revealed in the last time: they were kept by the power of God through faith, that after trial in the furnace they might be found unto praise, and honour, and glory at the appearing of Jesus Christ, whom having not seen they loved, in whom though then they saw him not, yet believing they rejoiced with joy unspeakable and full of glory, receiving the end of their faith, even the salvation of their souls, and looking forward to the completion of the work in the redemption of their bodies from the dominion of death. No wonder that the angels desire to look into these things.

In the second place, we learn from the Acts, 17th chapter, that the resurrection of Christ is to all men an assurance that God will judge the world in righteousness. In concluding his discourse to the Athenians, the Apostle says, " And the times of this ignorance God winked at; but now commandeth all men every where to repent: Because he hath appointed a day in the which he will judge the world in righteousness by that man whom he hath ordained, whereof he hath given *assurance* to all men in that he hath raised him from the dead." We are naturally led to inquire how the confidence is given, or what is the definite connexion betwixt the resurrection of Christ and the assurance of an equitable tribunal. We may ascertain this by glancing at the fifth chapter of John, from the 22d verse. " For the Father judgeth no man, but hath committed all judgment unto the Son: that all men should honour the Son, even as they honour the Father. He that honoureth not the Son honoureth not the Father which hath sent him. Verily, verily, I say unto you, he that heareth my word and believeth on him that sent me, hath everlasting life, and shall not come into condemnation, but is passed from death unto life. Verily, verily, I say unto you, the hour is coming and now is, when the dead shall hear the voice of the Son of God; and they that hear shall live. For as the Father hath life in himself, so hath he given to the Son to have life in himself; and hath given him authority to execute judgment also, because he is the Son of man. Marvel not at this, for the hour is coming in the which all that are in the graves shall hear his voice, and shall come forth; they that have done good, unto the resurrection of life, and they that have done evil, unto the resurrection of damnation." These were majestic claims from a being who was at that time wearing a tabernacle of flesh:—equality with God, power to transform the human heart, to raise the dead, and to judge the world in equity. Had the Saviour not been the being he represented himself—had he been an impostor, arrogating the attributes and power of God for purposes of delusion, the grave would have held the prisoner. For God would never have raised again a false pretender and bold blasphemer, who had staked the divinity of his mission on the very fact of a resurrection. Hence, if he had not been the Son of God, his sleep would have been eternal, unless it had been broken by horrid dreams, as the punishment of iniquity. But as he has been raised from the dead, all his pretensions are sustained, his work is marked with the broad seal of heaven, and all men may rest assured that there will be a righteous judgment: there will be a resurrection of the just, and a resurrection of the unjust. Blessed and holy is he that hath part in the *first* resurrection, on such the second death hath no power; but they are priests unto God and Christ, and reign with him a thousand years. Determine in the strength of God that the life and liberty of the first resurrection shall be yours, and avoid the unknown horrors of the second death.

In the third place, we learn from the Epistle of Paul to the Ephesians, first chapter, that the resurrection of Christ is to be a source of confidence as a bright illustration of the mighty power of God. " Wherefore, I also after I heard of your faith in the Lord Jesus, and love unto all the saints, cease not to give thanks for you, making mention of you in my prayers; that the God of our Lord Jesus Christ the Father of glory, may give unto you the spirit of wisdom and knowledge in the revelation of him: the eyes of your understanding being enlightened that ye may know what is the hope of his calling, and what the riches of the glory of his inheritance in the saints, and what is the exceeding greatness of his power to usward who believe, according to the working of his mighty power, which he wrought in Christ when he raised him from the dead, and set him at his own right hand in the heavenly places." When we look abroad through the world, and find that the fairest scenes have been laid waste by the ravages of sin, that the overwhelming majority of our race are still in the arms of the wicked one ; that war, covetousness, licentiousness, ignorance, superstition, infidelity, are all so rampant in society, that the material universe groans and labours in consequence of the crime and folly, the blood and tears of the moral agents who defile the great temple ; we are ready to inquire in spiritual pathos, When shall this despotism of evil come to an end ? By what power shall the government of Satan be shivered to pieces, and the tyranny of sin destroyed? The resurrection of Christ is the answer to the latter question. It gives us a glimpse of that omnipotent energy and infinite wisdom by which our risen Lord will ultimately subdue all things to himself. He has already defeated the dark counsels of fallen angels, has worsted and foiled death on his own dominions, has displayed how completely all elements and all beings are within the grasp of his immense power. So that believing this, we have the rock of ages to rest upon ;—we have the tranquil assurance, the joyous confidence, the unstaggering faith, that there are resources of might in reserve, by which the mastery of evil will for ever be put down, and the anguish of pain abolished. " Great and marvellous are thy works, Lord God Almighty, just and true are thy ways, thou King of saints. Who shall not fear thee, O Lord, and glorify thy name, for thou only art holy : for all nations shall come and worship before thee, for thy judgments are made manifest."* Such will be the song of Christ's victorious followers, when they stand upon the sea of glass mingled with fire, and awaken those thrilling and lofty melodies which belong

* Rev. 15th chap.

to the harps of God. Who is there that does not yearn to have a share in that victory, and a voice in that song."

I will now conclude the Lecture by a few general remarks. In the first place, the great advantage gained by insisting that Christianity is a religion of facts, is the following :—Facts cannot be overthrown by speculation. Deeds cannot be destroyed by reasoning; no class of metaphysical abstractions can annihilate the realities that have lived in the actual world, nor take away their meaning. It is vastly different with systems of intellectual and moral philosophy; there is continual flux and influx with them; they have their day and their adherents, and then are utterly abandoned. One system arises from the ashes of its predecessor, and is finally displaced by a third, which perishes in turn. But Christianity as a remedial system, is adapted to the unchanging necessities of humanity in every age, and in all stages. And being grounded on facts, resting upon things which were done, it has historic foundations, where supernatural light perpetually shines: for heaven and earth have come together, God and man have met at one, and time has been linked to the everlasting ages. Yes, the sandbanks raised by one wave of passion or speculation are washed away by another; but the Rock on which faith is anchored defies the tumult of every wave, and reposes in undisturbed majesty.

In the second place, by seeking the doctrine or meaning of the facts solely in the living oracles, we gain another great advantage: we avoid that black rock in creedland, where so many goodly vessels have struck and been broken to pieces. We find spiritual things explained in spiritual words. To the apostolic explication of the facts we will cling with heart and soul, nor bring ourselves into bondage by adherence to any human exposition. Human creeds are discordant and conflicting things; here the infidel has a wide field to travel in, and the antagonists are such that he can rush against them with overwhelming force. But let not any unbeliever mark out a course of that kind here. I will enter no such field: I would not weary myself by chasing phantoms, or hunting the spirit of a marsh;—the

Book, and nothing but the Book—Christianity as it came down from heaven, to be the life of the world.

The Lecture being concluded, it was announced by the Chairman, that all written questions courteously worded, and relevant to the subject, would be fairly and kindly examined. Upon which the following were handed in :—

1. Prove the resurrection of Christ; you have not settled that point.
2. Did not God authorise the Jews to destroy the seven tribes of Canaan, and if so, how can it be harmonized with justice or benevolence?
3. Was not the selection of Israel a manifestation of capricious partiality, and how can such partialities be reconciled with the character of a God who is said to love all the human family?
4. Does not ecclesiastical history prove that the Church was the chief agency of crime, darkness, and persecution during the middle ages? and if so, what has been the fruit of Christianity?

In reference to the first of these papers, I must remark that it is a statement and not a question. Patience is a virtue absolutely necessary in this world of ours, and I request the individual who handed in the remarks to wait until I come to the chapter of evidence. As the subject of each lecture has been announced, I will not anticipate a future evening by proving the resurrection: the remaining questions are equally irrevelant, but as an examination of two of them will save me the delivery of a distinct lecture in vindication of the Jewish dispensation, I will pay some attention to them.

To the question which seeks information about Canaan I reply: Yes! God authorised the destruction of Canaan, and it is in perfect harmony both with justice and benevolence. I will, in the first place, inquire into the justice of the deed by arranging the facts and considerations which belong to the subject.

1. He who is the supreme governor of the earth, to

whom the fulness of it belongs, promised to Abraham, for his devotion to truth and holiness in a time of general apostacy, that he and his seed should inherit the land of Canaan; this promise was often and solemnly repeated, but the most full account of it is contained in the 15th chapter of Genesis.—"I am the Lord that brought thee out of Ur of the Chaldees, to give thee this land to inherit it. And he said, Lord God, whereby shall I know that I shall inherit it? And He said unto him, take me an heifer of three years old, and a young pigeon, and a ram of three years old, and a turtle-dove. And he took unto him all these, and divided them in the midst, and laid each piece, one against another; but the birds divided he not. And when the fowls came down upon the carcases, Abraham drove them away. And, when the sun was going down, a deep sleep fell upon Abraham: And, lo! an horror of great darkness fell upon him. And He said unto Abraham, know of a surety that thy seed shall be a stranger in a land that is not theirs, and shall serve them. And they shall afflict them four hundred years. And also that nation whom they shall serve will I hide, and afterwards shall they come out with great substance. And thou shalt go to thy fathers in peace; thou shalt be buried in a good old age. But, in the fourth generation, they shall come hither again, for the iniquity of the Amorites is not yet full. And it came to pass that, when the sun went down, and it was dark, behold a smoking furnace, and a burning lamp, that passed between those pieces. In that same day, the Lord made a covenant with Abraham, saying, Unto thy seed have I given this land, from the river of Egypt to the great river, the river Euphrates." It appears, from this portion, that when the Lord made this covenant with Abraham, the iniquity of the original inhabitants was not full. God gives to nations, as to men, an opportunity of acting out their characters, and fulfilling their destinies, whether good or evil.

2. I will now inquire into the actual moral condition of the seven tribes of Canaan at the period of their visitation. By a reference to the 18th chapter of Leviticus, we find that the most foul, horrible, and almost unmen-

tionable vices, were generally prevalent. Idolatry, fornication, homicide, adultery, incest, sodomy, bestiality,—the prevalence of these vices had rendered each house a scene of squalor and discord, and each nation a theatre of licentiousness and carnage; hence the very land is represented as spueing them out, as the stomach disgorges some nauseating food or deadly poison:—" Defile not yourselves in any of these things, for in all these things the nations are defiled which I cast out before you. And the land is defiled, therefore I do visit the iniquity thereof upon it, and the land itself vomiteth out her inhabitants. Ye shall, therefore, keep my statutes and my judgments, and shall not commit any of these abominations, neither any of your own nation, nor any stranger that sojourneth among you,—for all these abominations have the men of the land done which were before you, and the land is defiled,—that the land spue not you out as it spued out the nations which were before you; for whosoever shall commit any of these abominations, even the souls that commit them, shall be cut off from among the people; therefore shall ye keep mine ordinances, that ye commit not any of these abominable customs which were committed before you, and that ye defile not yourselves therein. I am the Lord your God."

We distinctly see, from this portion of the word, that the Israelites and all their proselytes were to be punished with equal fierceness of indignation if they fell into the same unnatural depravity.

3. We are generally ready to discourse most eloquently concerning the rights of man, and man, no doubt, has rights which should be sacredly guarded, and inviolately preserved; but how strange it is that we so often forget the rights of God! our Creator, moral Proprietor, and Judge. If the creature has rights, surely the Creator must have them likewise; and, it may safely be asserted, that one of his most sacred and inviolable rights is, *the right of giving law where he has given life*, and, when his laws are broken, of inflicting those sanctions by which the laws are conserved and magnified. If we consider with seriousness and solemnity the high administration of God over the interests of heaven and earth, angels and men,—the majesty of the moral laws arising out of

the relation we sustain to him and to all created being,—his immaculate purity, and the consequent fearfulness and magnitude of sin,—we then discern in the facts under consideration the justice and righteous judgment of God, in the destruction of those who, by the most abominable crimes, were polluting the groaning earth, and hurling defiance against the majesty of heaven. The man of chastened and comprehensive mind, in surveying such a scene as the extermination of the Canaanites, never loses his reverence for the God of Israel, for over all and through all the physical horror of perishing humanity, dilapidated art, and desolate nature, he discerns the purifying operation of necessary penalties,—the sublime agency of moral retribution; and, with the nature of man, and the philosophy of history before us, we are well aware that if such retributive agency were not in existence, our earth might become a lost star, wandering in blackness of darkness.

I will conclude this branch of the subject by a quotation from the 9th chapter of Deuteronomy:—" Understand, therefore, this day, that the Lord thy God is he that goeth over before thee as a consuming fire; he shall destroy them, and he shall bring them down before thy face; so shalt thou drive them out, and destroy them quickly, as the Lord hath said unto thee. Speak not thou in thine heart after that the Lord thy God hath cast them out before thee, saying, For my righteousness the Lord hath brought me in to possess this land; but for the wickedness of these nations the Lord doth drive them out from before thee. Not for thy righteousness, or the uprightness of thine heart dost thou go to possess their land; but for the wickedness of these nations the Lord thy God doth drive them out from before thee; and that he may perform the word which he sware unto thy fathers, Abraham, Isaac, and Jacob."

But as even the sternest infliction of justice is benevolent when considered on a grand scale, I will now endeavour, in the second place, to show that there was mercy in the deed, as well as justice.

1. It was mercy to the Canaanites themselves. On this point I fear no criticism. I make my appeal to all

who know anything about natural laws, (and those who do not, may consult Mr Combe,) or the manner in which such laws would operate amid universal indulgence in infamous unnatural vices. The people generally would be monsters of passion, disease, deformity, and uncleanness, unfit, either in body or soul, to remain on the face of the earth,—they were the shame of creation. And even the pain connected with their destruction would merely be like dust in the balance if weighed against the intolerable agonies which, while living, they were enduring and inflicting on each other.

2. It was mercy to posterity. It prevented beings, unable to procreate a healthy offspring, from lengthening out a chain of burning torture, by the transmission of disease and death, and the propagation of murder,—it prevented them from heaving the filthy burden of their enormous turpitude upon the shoulders of another generation,—it dried up, out of the channel of time, a turbid and desolating torrent which might have withered every green and living thing, by rotting and blackening the verdure of the human race.

3. It was mercy to the Israelites. They had been enslaved in iron bondage for four hundred years, and endured a painful pilgrimage in the wilderness, that they might be fitted to enjoy, with grateful humility, the munificence of God. Hence we read in the 8th chapter of Deuteronomy:—"Thou shalt also consider in thine heart, that as a man chasteneth his son, so the Lord thy God chasteneth thee. Therefore thou shalt keep the commandments of the Lord thy God, to walk in his ways and to fear him. For the Lord thy God bringeth thee into a good land,—a land of brooks of water, of fountains, and depths that spring out of vallies and hills,—a land of wheat, and barley, and vines, and fig-trees, and pomegranates,—a land of oil, olive, and honey,—a land wherein thou shalt eat bread without scarceness, thou shalt not lack any thing in it." The remaining portion of the chapter develops the serious moral conditions upon which depended their continuance and peace in that prolific and beautiful land.

In the third place, I will proceed to show that such

retribution is in strict consonance with natural laws, or, in other words, that the penal inflictions recorded in the oracles of inspiration are analogous with the working of God as displayed in the material universe.

The natural theologian often enchants us by spreading before us the visible harmonies of nature. Spring arises in virgin beauty, and tripping in fairy grace over hill and valley, breathes her awakening lute, until the dark sleep of vegetation is broken up, and the unribbed waters rejoice in salient freedom. Voluptuous summer comes next, in the flush of ripeness, and the glow of exceeding splendour,—her voice like airs from heaven, —her breath like gales from paradise. Succeeded by matronly autumn,—majestic, yet furrowed with eld,— her bountiful hand pouring forth with profusion the mellow fruit and the golden grain. As her rich voice grows tremulous, stern winter usurps the scene, and from the throne of sterile gloom scatters the purifying tempest, and rolls the accumulating flood, until the languid earth recruits her exhausted energies, and replenishes her amazing stores. By this marvellous arrangement, the sustenance of life is provided for man and beast, and all whose hearts are not indurate rejoice in the bounty of God. If all the operations of nature were in manifest harmony to the eye of reason, we might conclude that the moral economy of the earth was unshattered, and man still basking in the unqualified approbation of the Divinity. But, then, we behold man the chief being in the earthly group, wasted away by lengthened disease, or suddenly hurried by dire calamity into silence and darkness. Cancer eats away its victim by atoms,—consumption drains away his vitality by stealth,—fever burns him into a skeleton of bones,—the varioloid putrifies him alive. The volcanic mountains belch forth their entrails, first blotting out the sun by dun sulphureous smoke, then lighting the temple of nature with unnatural glory, as the lava rivers of a symbolic hell arise up and rush forth in horrible devastation, burying towns or kingdoms, with all their life, glory, and magnificence. The earthquake utters her dreadful voice, causing the earth to undulate like the ocean shaken by the storm-blast,—an abyss opens out like the grave of nature, into which myriads of men, women, and children are precipitated, together with all the structures of their renown, and the records of their greatness, while oblivion, the high-priest, in withering mockery, performs the funeral ceremonies. The great deep bursts its barriers, and, like demons leaping on their prey, the wrathful waves lay waste the harvest of man's industry and hopes, sweeping away tens of thousands upon a voyage of discovery, from which they never return. The simoon of the desert awakens in sudden wrath, and sweeps on in tremendous force, burying in dreary ravines, or beds of suffocating sand, the travellers who were yearning for home, as the sick man yearns for the light and the incense of the morning. Famine invades the climes where a torrid sun darts intolerable rays, and the rains of heaven are withheld, until ghastly and ravenous beings, in haggard congregations, tear each other to pieces, and rave unheeded from the earth of iron to the heavens of brass. Then arises pestilence from the unburied dead or the noxious swamp, and, riding through the tainted air in a canopy of darkness, scatters among millions of beings in every clime such shapes of disease, and modes of death, as are too frightful for description.

If these things be so, the man who arrogantly rejects a miracle-vouched revelation, because it contains the records of severe retribution, can find no refuge in Deism. Nature, his own idol! laughs him to scorn from every land, and in every mood of irony. He must either give up his vain argument, or be driven into absolute Atheism, that pit in which there is not a drop of living water, nor a solitary ray of light.

The third question reads—Was not the selection of Israel a manifestation of capricious partiality, and how can such partialities be reconciled with the character of a God who is said to love all the human family?—I reply, that the selection of Israel was the result of all grasping benevolence, in union with all comprehending wisdom. The proof shall be forthcoming, Through a course of desperate iniquity, the nations and tribes of the earth had wandered far from the source of heaven's light. That most sublime and most influential of all ideas, the idea of God, was not retained in sanctifying power by the human family. Idolatry was almost universal, either in its milder or its more malignant forms. The luminaries of heaven and the reptiles of the earth, the great energies of nature, and the evil passions of the human heart, were all mounting into divinities, and receiving the homage of darkened souls. One grand design, then, for which God gave to himself a body in Israel was, that the knowledge of the living God might travel in brightness from one land to another, that there might be a central source of evidence and illustration, blazoning to all around the unity, power, love, and government of the Godhead. This was effectually done; for whatever the vices of the Israelites, yet the structure of their social system, and the character of their standing institutions, always bore evidence to the glory of God. In the second place, the Jewish nation was a depository for the prophetic word. To them were committed the oracles of God. Age after age, a number of holy seers were raised up in succession, to whom the glory of the future was unveiled, for the consolation of the pure, and the warning of the profane. As many of these prophecies contained minute predictions respecting things which were to transpire in the far distant future, it was necessary that their writings should be sacredly preserved. The providence of God is strikingly illustrated in the fact,—that whilst the Jews were actually staining their synagogues and temple with the blood of these holy men, yet at the same time they preserved and treasured their communications with religious care. We have these writings safe in our hands, and comparing them with the facts which have transpired and are transpiring, they constitute a body of conclusive evidence to the truth and authenticity of that Christianity which is the ground of our faith and the source of all our hope. In the third place, it was necessary that there should be a human line through which Christ should come according to the flesh, that he might be properly identified when he appeared in the world, as the Prophet, Priest, and King promised by God through all the prophets to rise out of a certain tribe, in a definite locality. This object was likewise realised by the separation and preservation of

Israel as a distinct and peculiar people. Bearing in mind these things, we find that the Israelites were merely a link in the chain of providence; their selection was not caprice or partiality, but the wisdom of God's working for purposes of universal benevolence. In the 43d chapter of Isaiah, we read as follows from the 9th verse: "Let all the nations be gathered together, and let the people be assembled, who among them can declare this and show us former things? Let them bring forth their witnesses, that they may be justified: or let them hear, and say, It is truth. Ye are my witnesses, saith the Lord, and my servant whom I have chosen: that ye may know and believe me, and understand that I am he; before me there was no God formed, neither shall there be after me. I, even I, am the Lord, and besides me there is no saviour. I have declared, and have saved, and I have showed, when there was no strange god among you, therefore ye are my witnesses, saith the Lord, that I am God." I earnestly recommend the entire chapter to your consideration; you will then see distinctly the past and present position of that remarkable people, and likewise have a glimpse of the glory of their future prospects. It appears, then, from this review of the destruction of Canaan, and the selection and settlement of Israel, that the whole work was a striking display of faithfulness, justice, wisdom, and love. Our own knowledge, faith, hope, and joy, arise in a great measure from tracing the connexion between the dispensations of divine wisdom.

The fourth question reads,—Does not ecclesiastical history prove that the Church of Christ was the chief agency of crime, darkness, and intolerance, during the middle ages? I reply, No! But as the answer is a very short one, it must be followed by some kind of an explanation. If any individual were accusing the English people, as a body, of gambling, plundering, and murderous propensities,—as a loyal and loving son of that land, I would demand some documentary evidence. But if the individual, in proof of his statement, began to read the Newgate Calendar, I would be inclined to cry out, stop! that's not the history of England! Yet the Newgate Calendar has as much claim to be the history of England as Ecclesiastical history has to be the history of the Church of Christ. Historians have been in such a dense fog, that they have confounded the Church with that dreadful corporation that embodied and perpetuated the Roman apostacy. During the long and dark reign of this gigantic system of iniquity, the few faithful men who constituted the *Church upon the rock* were in the dens and caves of the earth, in the heart of the gloomy wilderness, in the dungeons of the Inquisition; in short, in all those places which rendered the records of their history very scanty and fragmentary. The history of the Church remains to be written!

Having now answered all the questions which have been handed in, I may be allowed to conclude, as I feel much exhausted. I likewise beg leave to state, that for the future I must insist upon the questions being more relevant to the subject under consideration. God grant to you the nobility of mind to "prove all things, and hold fast that which is good."

THE END.

Printed by Libri Plureos GmbH in Hamburg,
Germany